Working Dogs

K-9 Police Dogs

by Mari Schuh

Consulting Editor: Gail Saunders-Smith, PhD

Consultant: Officer David Dewey, K-9 Unit,
Colchester Police Department, Colchester, Vermont

CAPSTONE PRESS
a capstone imprint

Pebble Plus is published by Capstone Press,
151 Good Counsel Drive, P.O. Box 669, Mankato, Minnesota 56002.
www.capstonepub.com

032010
005740CGF10

 Books published by Capstone Press are manufactured with paper
containing at least 10 percent post-consumer waste.

Library of Congress Cataloging-in-Publication Data
Schuh, Mari C., 1975–
    K-9 police dogs / by Mari Schuh.
    p. cm.—(Pebble plus. Working dogs)
    Includes bibliographical references and index.
    Summary: "Simple text and full-color photos illustrate the traits, training, and duties of K-9 police dogs"—
Provided by publisher.
    ISBN 978-1-4296-4470-9 (library bindiing)
    1. Police dogs—Juvenile literature. I. Title. II. Series.
HV8025.S39 2011
363.2—dc22   2009051414

Editorial Credits
Erika Shores, editor; Bobbie Nuytten, designer; Marcie Spence, media researcher; Eric Manske, production specialist

Photo Credits
Capstone Studio/Karon Dubke, cover (collar), 1, 5, 11, 15, 19, 21
Courtesy of Officer David Dewey of Colchester Police Department, 9
Mark Raycroft, cover
Newscom, 7, 17
Shutterstock/Cherkas, 13

Note to Parents and Teachers

The Working Dogs series supports national social studies standards related to people, places,
and culture. This book describes and illustrates K-9 police dogs. The images support early
readers in understanding the text. The repetition of words and phrases helps early readers
learn new words. This book also introduces early readers to subject-specific vocabulary words,
which are defined in the Glossary section. Early readers may need assistance to read some
words and to use the Table of Contents, Glossary, Read More, Internet Sites, and Index sections
of the book.

Table of Contents

Fighting Crime

Police K-9s are four-legged
crime fighters.
These brave dogs help
the police.

Police dogs chase criminals.

They also search

for missing people.

Police dogs sniff for drugs and bombs. They scratch at the spot where they find drugs. They sit down where they find bombs.

The Right Kind of Dog

Police dogs are outstanding dogs.

They always follow commands.

An excellent sense of smell

helps them do their job.

Male German shepherds
make good police dogs.
They are strong, smart,
and aggressive.

K-9 police dog in training

Training

Police dogs begin training after their first birthday. They learn commands. They search for smells and are rewarded with a toy.

On the Job

Police dogs patrol streets
with police officers.
These dogs climb stairs
and jump over walls.

Police dogs wear
vests for protection.
They are called tactical vests.

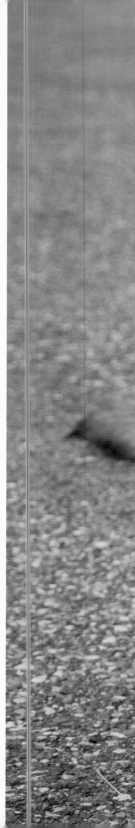

Police dogs work

for about six to eight years.

They fight crime with

the police every day.

Glossary

aggressive—strong and forceful; male German shepherds are naturally aggressive; their police dog training keeps them from being too aggressive

command—an order to follow a direction

criminal—a person who breaks the law

patrol—to walk or travel around an area to protect it or to keep watch on people

reward—to give something for a job well done

tactical vest—a piece of equipment worn to protect people or animals during times of danger

Read More

Bozzo, Linda. *Police Dog Heroes.* Amazing Working Dogs. Berkeley Heights, N.J.: Enslow Publishers, 2010.

Murray, Julie. *Crime-Fighting Animals.* Going to Work. Edina, Minn.: Abdo Pub., 2009.

Internet Sites

FactHound offers a safe, fun way to find Internet sites related to this book. All of the sites on FactHound have been researched by our staff.

Here's all you do:

Visit *www.facthound.com*

FactHound will fetch the best sites for you!

Index

Word Count: 141
Grade: 1
Early-Intervention Level: 16